MY SEXUALITY MY UNIQUENESS.
knowing your sexuality and how to embrace it without compromise.

By Verlaine Harts

Table of contents

chapter One : Identify your sexual
Sexuality covers an expansive range and is likewise profoundly private. It's tied in with understanding the sexual sentiments and attractions we feel towards others, not who we end up having intercourse with. There are various sorts of sexuality, and it can require investment to sort out what fits right with you. If somebody is giving you trouble about your sexuality, figure out what to do and who you can converse with.

You are what is going on, so don't feel like you want to do or say anything that puts others' requirements before yours. It's completely dependent upon you whether, when, and how you share your contemplations on your sexuality.

As opposed to feeling like you need to declare precisely who and what you distinguish as, you can simply discuss where your head's at and your opinion on sexuality, and take individuals on an excursion with you.

I'm prepared to talk - yet how would I have the discussion?
Assuming that you're prepared to emerge or welcome in, there are things to remember:

Contemplate how you will care for yourself after the discussion. You should rest and enjoy a show that praises the strange local area, or maybe you'll interview with a help administration.

Be clear with yourself about who you're prepared to impart to.
Tell those individuals what you want from them. Do you need them essentially to tune in, share their encounters, proposition guidance or backing, or even assist you with conversing with others?

Give yourself the time you want to have this talk - you would rather not feel rushed or hurried.

Plan what you're venturing out in front of time so you feel as sure as could be expected.

Permit individuals to be astonished. Allow them to handle the data, and recall that it might take more than one discussion.

Know that the first response won't endure all the time. You may not get the response you need, however that doesn't mean it will constantly be like that.

Assuming somebody responds adversely, be patient yet recall that you can leave. You don't need to cop unfortunate treatment, so get yourself out of the circumstance assuming you want to.

There's nobody size-fits-all way to deal with these things, so what has worked for others may not work for you. It depends on you to discover some way of taking care of it - to conclude how it affects your life and how you in the end decide to recognize it. There's no set-in-stone manner to be you, and you're presently well en route to praising what makes you special

Managing individuals who could do without your sexuality

It's critical to perceive that we as a whole are unique and that the things that vibe ideal for us are not the same as the things that vibe appropriate for another person. We ought to be conscious of and positive about others' sexuality or sexual connections and back their entitlement to investigate their sexuality in a protected, consensual and dependable way.

On the off chance that you want assistance?

It's never acceptable for somebody to irritate you or cause you to genuinely regret your sexuality. You never need to manage this sort of treatment from others all alone. Various administrations can offer you support assuming you're being irritated or harassed because of your sexuality.

Sorts of sexuality

Individuals utilize a couple of normal marks to recognize their sexuality. Your sexuality isn't characterized by who you have intercourse with - it's about how you feel and how you decide to recognize yourself. Significantly, you pick what mark feels good, or you pick no name by any means. You could find, in the same way as other others have, that the name you pick changes over the long haul.

Straight/Heterosexual

Drawn in generally to individuals of the other gender or orientation.

Gay/Homosexual

Drawn in generally to individuals of similar sex or orientation (alludes to folks - and frequently to young ladies, as well).

Lesbian

Drawn in for the most part to individuals of similar sex or orientation (alludes to ladies).

Bisexual+

A comprehensive term that portrays being drawn to heartfelt and additionally sexual accomplices of more than one orientation or sex. Certain individuals locally favor the term pansexual, which by and large depicts being drawn to all genders or sexes, and others locally may lean toward the term strange.

Polysexual

Drawn to heartfelt and sexual accomplices of numerous however not all sexes, genders, or sexual characters. ('Poly' signifies 'many'.)

Agamic

Not exactly physically drawn to anybody.

Certain individuals likewise pick the names 'eccentric' or 'liquid' as an approach to communicating their thoughts by their very own sentiments.

Your sexuality can confound

Sit back and relax if you don't know about your sexuality. Being youthful is a period for sorting out what works for you. Investigating and overseeing unmistakable inclinations is many times part of the experience. Whatever is going on, addressing and investigating your sexual character can be confounding and unnerving. You may be stressed over how your loved ones will respond, or how it affects your future. It's memorable's critical that, while it could feel overpowering, you're more than fit for overcoming this extreme period - and it won't endure forever.

On the off chance that you're prepared to emerge or welcome in, there are things to remember:

Ponder how you will take care of yourself after the discussion. You should rest and enjoy a show that commends the eccentric local area, or maybe you'll interview with a help administration.

Be clear with yourself about who you're prepared to impart to.

Tell those individuals what you want from them. Do you need them just to tune in, to share their encounters, deal guidance or backing, or even assist you with conversing with others?

Give yourself the time you want to have this visit - you would rather not feel rushed or hurried.
Plan what you're venturing out in front of time so you feel as sure as could be expected.

Permit individuals to be astounded. Allow them to handle the data, and recall that it might take more than one discussion.

Know that first response won't endure all of the time. You may not get the response you need, however that doesn't mean it will continuously be like that.

Assuming somebody responds adversely, be patient yet recall that you can leave. You don't need to cop unfortunate treatment, so get yourself out of the circumstance on the off chance that you want to.

Chapter two: Does my sexuality define me?

Everybody is unique. This is an undeniable assertion, I know. However, what's somewhat more subtle is the comprehension that we want to acknowledge one another, regardless of whether we like it. This applies to essentially all that somebody could be oppressed for, yet for this situation, I'm discussing sexuality. A lot of legislative issues become possibly the most important factor when the word 'sexuality' is raised, however, I'm not in any event, discussing political freedoms. I'm discussing somebody's on the right track to be adored, somebody's more right than wrong to be regarded and not judged, and somebody's on the whole correct to feel great in their skin.

Homosexuality is concerned shows that there's a developing acknowledgment currently in the event. Notwithstanding, you don't need to concur with homosexuality. I'm telling you however that nobody can settle on choices for another person. Nobody understands what others are going through, we as a whole are people encountering various things as the world keeps on turning. I accept one of the main things is to acknowledge individuals for what their identity is. Presently, I'm not expressing feel free to become friends with a crazy chronic executioner. That is not the thing I mean. I'm alluding to the way that another person's sexuality ought to hurt you not the slightest bit. Except if they're an attacker or kid molester, sexuality doesn't have anything to do with the nature of an individual. Individuals of all kinds of sorts of sexual direction are as yet human. I'm human, you perusing this is a human, individuals lounging around you are likewise human (except if you're distant from everyone else, except you get the point). We are generally similar species, we as a whole merit equivalent regard. So I for one accept that all people should be acknowledged. As expressed previously, if you disagree with an LGBT person's sexuality, then fine, remain quiet about it. There's a compelling reason need to cut others down, and how they manage their adoration life doesn't influence you. Sexuality isn't about who you engage in sexual relations with, or how frequently you have it. Sexuality is about your sexual sentiments, contemplations, attractions, and ways of behaving towards others. You can find others truly, physically, or sincerely appealing, and everything is a piece of your sexuality.

Sexuality is different and individual, and it is a significant piece of what your identity is. Finding your sexuality can be a very freeing, invigorating, and positive experience.

Certain individuals experience segregation because of their sexuality. On the off chance that somebody gives you trouble about your sexuality, it's great to converse with somebody about it. Correspondence and independence from segregation are crucial basic freedoms that have a place with all individuals.

In many states in Australia, including Victoria, it is illegal to oppress somebody on account of their sexual direction, orientation personality, or legal sexual movement. Be that as it may, separation can in any case happen.

Chapter Three: Should i be scared of my sexuality?

Today, sexuality is by all accounts a region as private and loaded up with dread as ever it was. You could contend the inverse because such a great amount about sexuality these days is valiantly open — and that is valid if by "public" you mean the only noticeable. Yet, secretly, we haven't progressed far in that frame of mind to discuss our sexuality, one with another.

As in a long time ago, we leave on our sexual excursions with negligible direction — zip, truly. There's the sparse conversation about being a sexual being: how it feels, what we do, who we are physically, and how that affects us as we approach our lives. We don't have a lot of thought about what sex is for, even. (If it were exclusively for propagation, wouldn't we groove occasionally like different vertebrates?) Rarely can couples in long-haul connections extend the extent of their common arousing quality? Psychotherapy has gone from surveying sex supernaturally, as

 a lot of contemporary psychotherapy appears to have limited sexuality to something like a component of a relationship, as opposed to power in itself, a domain all its own.

Imagine a scenario where "overfamiliarity" is a cover for something different. Imagine a scenario where that "something different" is dread. Apprehension about the power that falsehoods holding up in the risky spots you might go in the domain of your faculties, where you've been maintaining mysteries from your reality and your sweetheart, however from yourself?

You can be seeing someone years and out of nowhere see a face upon your darling that you've never seen and never speculated was there. Gradually I understood that it wasn't "like" my body changed physically with various individuals and various circumstances; it changed. People are such strong receptors and radiators that you change what I'd call your "imaginal body" in sexual closeness with another, and different changes thusly. This is such a long way from the model of sexuality introduced by and to standard society that it required me an investment to engage the thought that maybe it was society as a rule, and not me, that was physically shocking. Society says you're one of several things — male or female, straight or gay, youthful or old, human or creature. Yet, the further you adventure into the domain of the faculties, the more you experience the shape-moving truth of your in-betweenness in sentiments and impressions that are male and female, straight and gay, youthful and old, human and creature. This can get quite befuddling.

Indeed, on the off chance that I'm a hetero eccentric, I know a certain something: regardless of how weird your experience is, regardless of how exceptional it feels, you're by all accounts not the only one having such an encounter.

Sexuality is alarming because it's where we meet ourselves most straightforwardly, without channels, without verbiage, and, assuming we go adequately far, without fixed jobs. It's where we meet ourselves with and through the Other — this Other with whom we venture into the domain; this Other, an accomplice as the liquid.

Chapter Four: Accepting my sexuality

I get that this presumably seems like a tiny and clear thing, yet I truly think this is an opinion that we don't communicate enough. This assertion alone envelops such countless significant sentiments that I hold exceptionally near my sexual character today. Your sexuality is your own, and no other person's. This excursion is about you and getting to know yourself. It tends to be hard to isolate ourselves from the cross-section of connections and impacts that we experience consistently, yet that is the reason making yourself the center is so significant. Your character isn't for any other person, ever - it's for yourself and you alone to deal with, embrace and express any way you like.

A large portion of us limits our time spent stripped down, in many cases out of disgrace, humiliation, or frailty. The body is normal, practical, and astounding. Appreciating those characteristics ought not to be any. The additional time you spend exposed, the more agreeable you will accompany the thought and, undoubtedly, with your body. Check out yourself before the mirror. Attempt to take out body-negative considerations and attempt to zero in on what you love about yourself. This can assist with molding you to see yourself in a more certain light.

Who cares about sexuality? It summons such profound reactions at whatever point it is raised. Sexuality is introduced in limits in our way of life: possibly you're a "spouse material" (or husband material) or have "to an extreme" sexual longing. Possibly you are a "prig" or a "whore." It's no big surprise ladies are so confounded there are blended messages wherever we turn. This makes it hard for ladies to embrace our bodies and communicate our thoughts physically in a non-critical, positive way.

Being gay is harder to grapple with than hairlessness, obviously, in light of society's perspectives. You don't loathe yourself; you have inactively consumed others' negative perspectives. Religion is essential for society, and when it enters what is happening, one breeze up with one more layer of objection — may be the most extreme of all — because to be gay, as per Christian fundamentalists, is to place your spirit in danger.

Self-judgment and weakness

Cures: Find one thing I am great at, get together with individuals who esteem my achievements, track down a comrade to discuss my thoughts with, befriend someone who can act as a model or guide

Strict responsibility

Cures: Read a book on present-day confidence and gay resilience, find a gay companion who is likewise Christian, search out a gay minister

Sexual disappointment

Cures: Join a gay gathering that is tied in with something other than sex (climbing, films, moving, leisure activities), read about legends and trailblazers of gay freedom, and relate major areas of strength to models who have effectively consolidated sex and love

Fortunately, this can be fixed. It doesn't make any difference what your position on sex is, or whether you're seeing someone. At the point when everything reduces, sexuality is truly about embracing yourself in each viewpoint mind, body, and soul. It's tied in with tracking down your appealing characteristics and feeling sure about them.

Chapter Five :How to live a normal life as LGBTQ

Business separation, alongside segregation in lodging and medical services, is quite normal in the LGBTQ people group. It can hinder LGBTQ individuals' capacity to accomplish and keep up with monetary security. That is the reason LGBTQ individuals' approach must uphold that assist them with putting food on the table, access medical services, and putting a rooftop over their heads. Notwithstanding the significant requirement for public advantages in the LGBTQ people group, admittance to these advantages is not even close to guaranteed.

While research has shown that individuals from the LGBTQ people group report lower earnings and higher paces of destitution, expanded food uncertainty, higher joblessness, and more noteworthy weakness to vagrancy than the general population,3 extra examinations are expected to inspect LGBTQ individuals' receipt of the scope of critical advantages that might end up being useful to resolve those issues. The new Center for American Progress study information investigated in this report utilizes a broadly delegate test of both LGBTQ-distinguished and non-LGBTQ-recognized grown-ups to extend the comprehension of the degree to which the LGBTQ people group gets specific advantages and decide if differences exist based on LGBTQ character and other segment factors. Coming out is a course of understanding, tolerating, and esteeming your sexual direction/character. It includes both investigating your personality and offering your character to other people. Coming out can be a progressive cycle or one that is extremely unexpected. The initial step for the most part includes emerging to yourself, frequently with an acknowledgment that sentiments you've had for quite a while seem OK on the off chance that you can characterize them as gay, lesbian, sexually open, transsexual, or eccentric.

Coming out can be an undeniably challenging cycle. Our general public unequivocally authorizes codes of conduct concerning the sexual direction and orientation personality, and a great many people get the message that they should be hetero and act as indicated by society's meaning of their orientation. For gay, lesbian, and sexually unbiased people, there might be a feeling of being unique or of not fitting into the jobs expected of you by your family, companions, work environment, or more prominent society. Coming out includes confronting cultural reactions and mentalities toward LGBTQ individuals. You might feel embarrassed, secluded, and apprehensive.

Albeit coming out can be troublesome, it can likewise be a very freeing and liberating process. You might feel like you can at long last be real and consistent with what your identity is. You might find an entire local area of individuals like you and feel upheld and propelled. Regardless of whether it's terrifying to contemplate emerging to other people, once in a while the prize can merit the test that approaching out involves.

People don't travel through the approaching out process at a similar speed. The cycle is exceptionally private. It occurs in various ways and happens at various ages for various individuals. Certain individuals know about their sexual personality at an early age, and others show up at this mindfulness after numerous years. Coming out is a proceeding, in some cases long-lasting, process.

When you acknowledge that you're lesbian, gay, sexually open, transsexual, or strange, you can choose to be out to other people or to remain "in the wardrobe." You are the main individual who can choose when and how it is protected to emerge. You might choose to turn out in one piece of your life and not in another. For instance, certain individuals are out to their families yet in the storeroom at work; certain individuals are out at school yet in the storage room with their families. For gay, lesbian, sexually unbiased, transsexual, and strange individuals approaching our interaction can be both troublesome and freeing. For the vast majority, it requires investment to know what your identity is. It is OK to be confounded or to be dubious about whether or how to emerge. Keep in mind, that you are in good company. There are numerous others with very different kinds of feedback that you have. There are additionally individuals and associations that can support or guide you. It's vital to find the assistance you with requiring from the assets accessible to you.